F
OF T

EDMUND ENGLISH

KULVERT
NEWCASTLE UPON TYNE

FATIMA OF THE HILLS

dedicated to
Sharif Rkhaoui Simohamed,
Berber horseman of the beach

'Who is this that cometh out of the wilderness like pillars of smoke, perfumed with myrrh and frankincense, with all powders of the merchant?'

- Song of Solomon 3:6

FLIGHT FROM THE DESERT

herded like Amazonian cattle
brought to the slaughter
for fatty fried burgers

one flies every minute
herbal brew of Jasmine tea
buy your VAT free sexy underwear

you can't tax a fuck
watching ramen noodles
slurp out of people's mouths

waitress's legs are too skinny
and sky is hazy like a desert
flight centre a Foucauldian tower

there's no escaping the draconian eye
armed guards hustle you at the entrances
time is a jet plane as you wait to fly

mountains become clouds
and clouds become mountains
only the clear blue mirrors your mind

planes leave a trail of human excess
guilty of the greenhouse gasses
not even a camel ride is ethical

teethy smile meets you at the taxi rank
bundled into the back of a dark car
zooming through the busy streets

with mopeds darting rush and beep
French tourists bustle in the avenues
stray cats flee as the cars scrape by

two lovers talk Parisian gossip
on the terrace, first sip of tea is a blessing
Atthé on the balcony over the square

drumbeats of smoking Berber loneliness
or how not to be alone on desert nights
Ali Baba, you Ali Baba as he strokes my beard

better than the Franks thinking I'm Daniel
Radcliffe.

14

HAPPY BIRTHDAY HOUSSEN

Seeing in my 30th, I'm drunk on the fringes of
the medina with two Royal Navy contractors,
one from Plymouth, one from County Durham,
who have flown in from the rock of Gibraltar.

I can't escape the English.
They go quiet when discussing their work.
I imagine them arresting immigrant ships
sailing with blind hope from Africa.

I have shared the day with a beautiful
Singaporean New Yorker blessed
with intricate Henna designs on her hands.
As the Isha prayer calls, I arrive at her hotel.

We watch Spanish flamenco music
in a bar that serves Western alcohol.
TV screens blare late-night images
of bikini-clad girls on the beach.

It's too loud as I watch the sailors
hit on the New Yorker.
As the night slips away from me
our guide, a man from the desert,

later takes her to a brothel.

KAFTANS AND MINARETS

Galloping along the beach
sea spray as I hold onto the saddle
riding at speed feeling
the vivacity of the female barb.

In the stable the fragrance
of the Arab and the Arabian,
greys and browns, dirt fur
and sweet hum of wet hay.

Back in the Medina, the sensation
of the Daqqa, goatskin drums,
and the snake charmer's
carved apricot wood for his Ghayta.

Murmuration of birds
their song like Muezzin Prayer,
as the sun sets on the sea,
fried fish wafts in the salt air.

PURGE AND PURIFY

Down from the arid mountain
the prophets, the partitions, and the prayers
she who foretells the future, Kahina the Jew.

For Achoura, giving alms to the poor
lofty daily prayer at Koutoubia Mosque
with great ardour for the sanitary God.

The same God of sanctity exalted
by Jews coming back to Essaouira
blessed with aromas of hash.

Bedevilled Berber horse that I fall from
caked blood and the healing sound of guembri
scented hot oils in steaming massages

aching smell of iodine for my wounds.

REFLECTIONS OF OLD RAMON

I have drunk so much tea
I didn't make it to Tangier
with a tanned skin boy

but it's Rimbaud's birthday
and I'm reading de Nerval
slave girls for the Arabs

darkest skin with inner light
Yemenite children of Sheba
blackest of queens for Solomon

gifts of blue patterned ceramics
jewelled hands, backward glances
leather pouches, hash handouts

and talking hoopoe birds.

The mosque is an oasis
erect in the desert sun
I miss brewing my Darjeeling tea

in three simple minutes
watching the turquoise
salt of time slowly run out

listening to Mariana Flores
floating voice sing Barbara Strozzi
with a velvet sensual aroma

allowing Red House Painters
to wash over me, carving me
a new soul bled from the river.

It's a shame my shame,
I can't stand with conviction
for the things I've done.

INVADING MOORS

Palm trees are *shirk* idols in the dirt
stoic faith in the proud mule
born to constant servitude.

Stoned Juba II, the Berber ruler
watching the Numidian Crane
nest on the palace in the Medina.

Filth of the backstreets
informs the stray cat's instinct
to smartly avoid my camera.

Aroma of Morocco
hits you in the heat
spiced rotting leather.

Rkhaoui Simohamed,
the man in his Jellaba
pilgrim pointed hood

crafting his trade.

HEY YOU! ALI BABA!

Hustled in the Jewish quarter, I arrive at the synagogue but it is closed for prayer. A tap on my shoulder says *I'm no guide, no money, just live here* I give him my faith and he leads me to the spice market. The spice merchant picks a handful of produce from each sack on show, *smell this my friend, how'd you say in English? mint, cedar, good for home perfume, frankincense like bible, aniseed, here see Moroccan tooth pick, tea, royal tea!* He then leads me inside where jars upon jars of spices and scents are on show. A French couple are bartering over prices. He sits me down and brings me hot tea, I didn't intend to buy anything but I'm enjoying the mint tea, it's refreshing, so I enquire. *Royal tea?* He brings me a large bag of tea, *17 dirham* he says, I give him a 20 note. *No, no! 17, one seven!* I pull out a 100, he looks at it and says *50 more*. I'm calculating, I think I'm paying fifteen quid for tea. I want to leave so I give him the money. Enough tea to last a year. I head for the synagogue and another man stops me. *I show you the way.* He takes me to a sea of Jewish white slab graves, where tourists are taking photos and selfies amongst the memorials, all happening whilst a corner of Jews pray solemnly. Leaving the graveyard, it becomes sanctified by washing your hands at the exit, I follow the guide who leads me to the synagogue. He is telling me how Muslims and Jews live side by side, and that he has always lived in the Mellah. I pay his fee and leave.

After a visit to the contemporary art museum, which was a beautiful palace spoilt by tourist art, a man stops me as I try to visit the mosque. *It is closed for refurbishment,* he tells me, *but last day for the tanners. I practice my English on you, no money, no guide but you must see the Tanners, it's a great visit!* As we stroll and talk about football, he is more passionate about boxing, *Anthony Joshua! Tyson Fury!* He leads me down backstreets to the Tanners. It stinks to high heaven, smells worse than a rubbish dump, the air full of dead meat and shit. Vats of bubbling dead animals. Another tourist is called over *so you've been caught too!* I jest. The tanner gives me mint leaves to hold next to my nose, to hide the smell as we walk to a leather shop.

leather shop. After a quick tour, another couple of old women tourists have been trapped. I tell the proprietors I am not interested in buying leather bags, and I leave. The tanner demands payment and I harshly refuse, mainly because I feel nauseous from the heat and the stench. Later a man throws a snake around my head, asking for a photo, I quickly throw it off and hop into the nearest café. I order a mint tea and try and relax. I thought about throwing the snake back in his face and rescuing the dancing monkey he had on a chain. Instead, I read Gérard de Nerval as the sun sets, Journey to the Orient, tales of hashish adventures as the Muslim Adhan prayer rings out across the Place Jemaa el-Fna.

חלקת
תינוקות של בית רבן
תנצב"ה

LOVE, HOPE AND WORSHIP

I watch with dingy belief
slave musicians from Mali
entertain the colonial expats.

I move the food around my plate
with soiled touch. Fish bones
cling to my palate.

Liquefied silver poured into moulds
for decorative jewellery like red wine
into my empty glass.

What is fair? To radiantly set free
the barbary ape, as Bilal was liberated
by Muhammad?

His gift for curing Fatima.

HOME TO HIGH ATLAS

Do you give your faith
to every stranger that you meet
our existence is based on trust

so much life behind her eyes
animated peacock on parade
curved tea leaf eye lashes

soft girl with sharpest of minds
on top of the mosque minaret
white storks make a nest

bedding themselves in
with the holy call to prayer
bus to Ksar of Ait Ben Haddou

woven fabric maps the mountains
stained with dye of poppies
desert cactus and camel hair

Bedouins trade with the Jews
Jews trade with the Berbers
and the Arabs ride over the mountains

bringing Fatima, Maryam and Isa
translating the Koran and Kasbah
big building with four corners

clay baked fortified Tighremt
cold in day, warm at night
not a sign of rain

rivers crack dry day and night
salt crystals cling to the debris
red earth clay that we came from

prophets of trade, prophets of deserts
mountains shimmer grey with dust
strike out of the Sahara

flecks of a green oasis
shepherds draw lines in the dirt
a map of the heavens

tired donkeys are tied to the dust
dogs skirt the edges of town
with a limp for a scrap of meat

birches and pomegranates
grow at the edges of the river
scattering, flecks of cacti

piles of stones sprayed white
the road constantly collapses
lonely stray dog barks at us

fur white as the mountain tops
his soul dewy with sadness
an elder woman carries the toil

her back bowed
by the weight
of sheared maize.

OTHER BOOKS BY
KULVERT

Special thanks to Koef Nielsen for all of the advice and support that made this book possible.

Cover and inside photographs by the author.

First published in Great Britain
September 2024 by Kulvert
Second edition January 2025

ISBN 978 1 0685200 2 0

Second Edition KV-004

This book is printed entirely on recycled paper.

kulvertbooks.com